BLS Statistics By Occupation

United States workers held over 130 million jobs in May 2013—but what kind of jobs were they? Over 21 million were office and administrative support jobs, including 2.8 million general office clerks and 2.4 million customer service representatives. Another 14 million jobs were in sales occupations, primarily retail salespersons and cashiers, and nearly 12 million jobs were in food service occupations. Although most of the largest occupations were low paying, STEM (science, technology, engineering, and mathematics) jobs and other occupations requiring postsecondary education often had much higher wages. This Spotlight on Statistics uses data from the Occupational Employment Statistics program to provide an overview of occupational employment and wages in May 2013, with an emphasis on STEM jobs and occupational data by typical entry-level education required.

Nationwide, nearly 8 million retail salespersons and cashiers

Ten occupations accounted for more than 1 in every 5 jobs in May 2013. Two sales occupations—retail salespersons and cashiers—were the largest individual occupations, with employment of 4.5 million and 3.3 million, respectively. The largest occupations also included combined food preparation and serving workers, waiters and waitresses, registered nurses, and general office clerks.

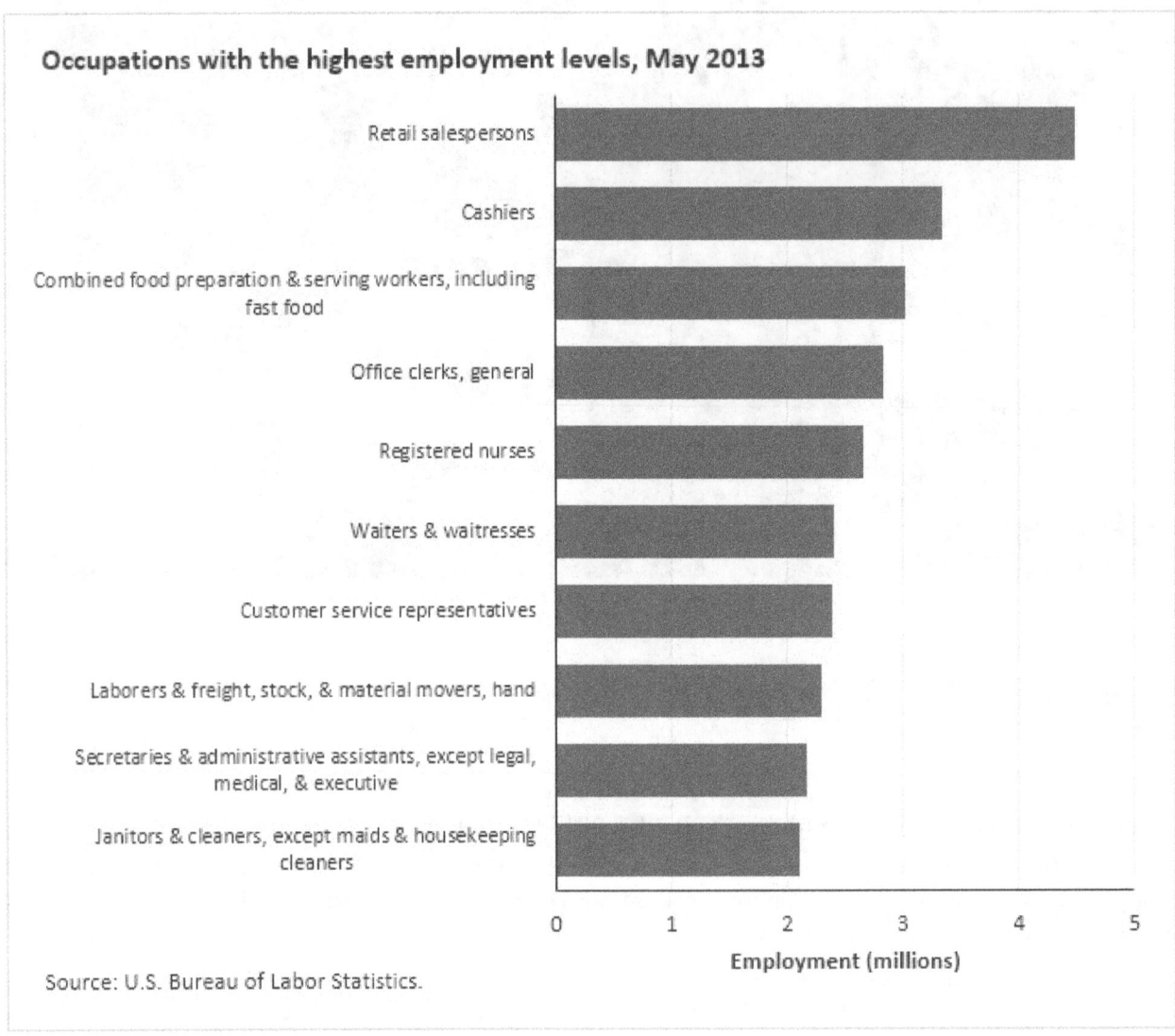

Source: U.S. Bureau of Labor Statistics.

Below-average wages for most of the largest occupations

Of the 10 largest occupations, only registered nurses had an average wage above the U.S. all-occupations mean of $46,440, and three occupations—combined food preparation and serving workers, including fast food; cashiers; and waiters and waitresses—were among the lowest paying occupations overall.

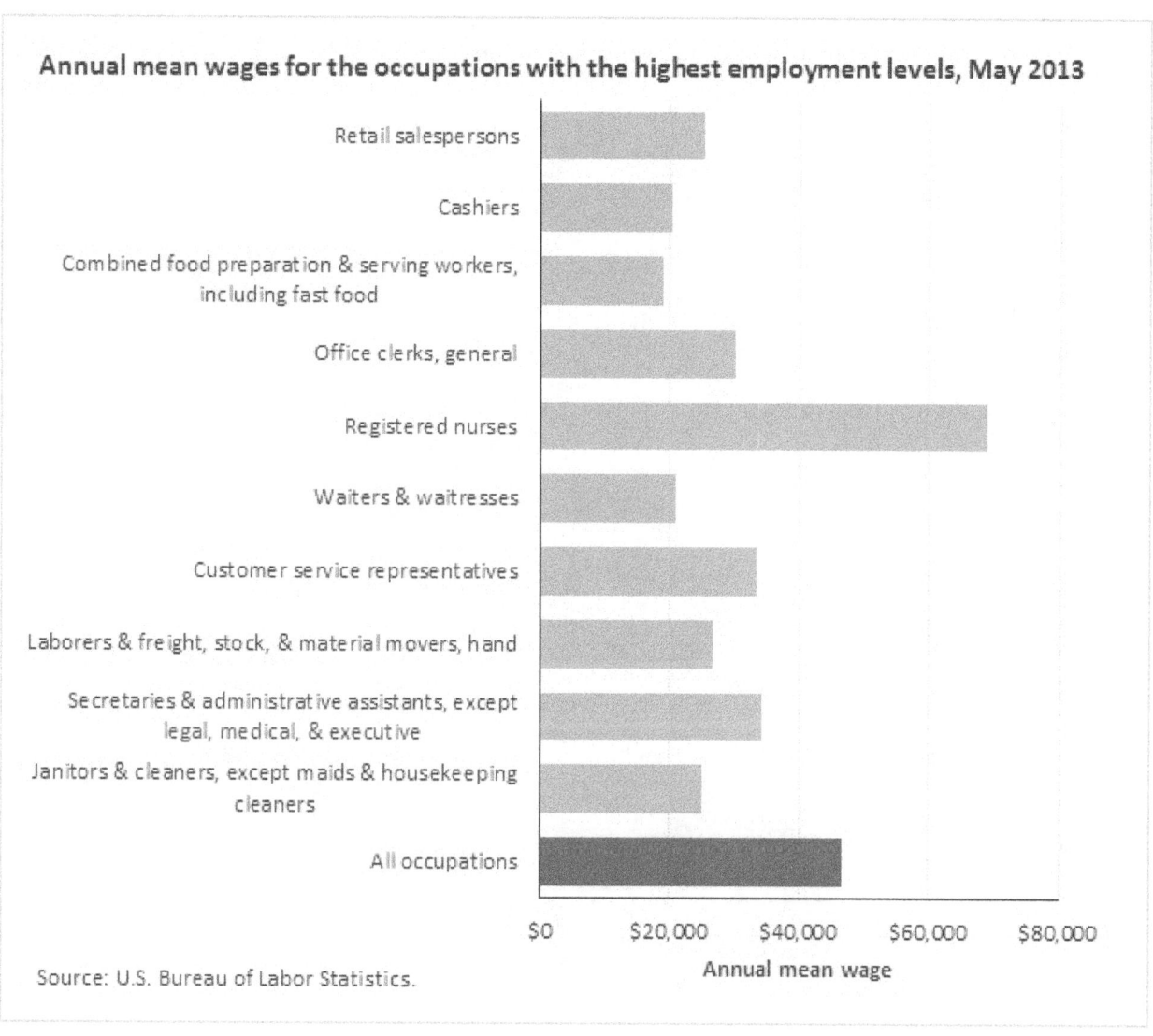

Office and administrative support occupations made up 1 of every 6 jobs

About 36 percent of jobs were in office and administrative support, sales, or food preparation and serving occupations. The smallest occupational groups included legal occupations and life, physical, and social science occupations, each representing less than 1 percent of total employment.

Food preparation and serving related occupations was the lowest paying occupational group, with an annual mean wage of $21,580. Other low-paying occupational groups included personal care and service and farming, fishing, and forestry. Management, legal, and computer and mathematical occupations were the highest paying occupational groups.

Employment and annual mean wages by occupational group, May 2013

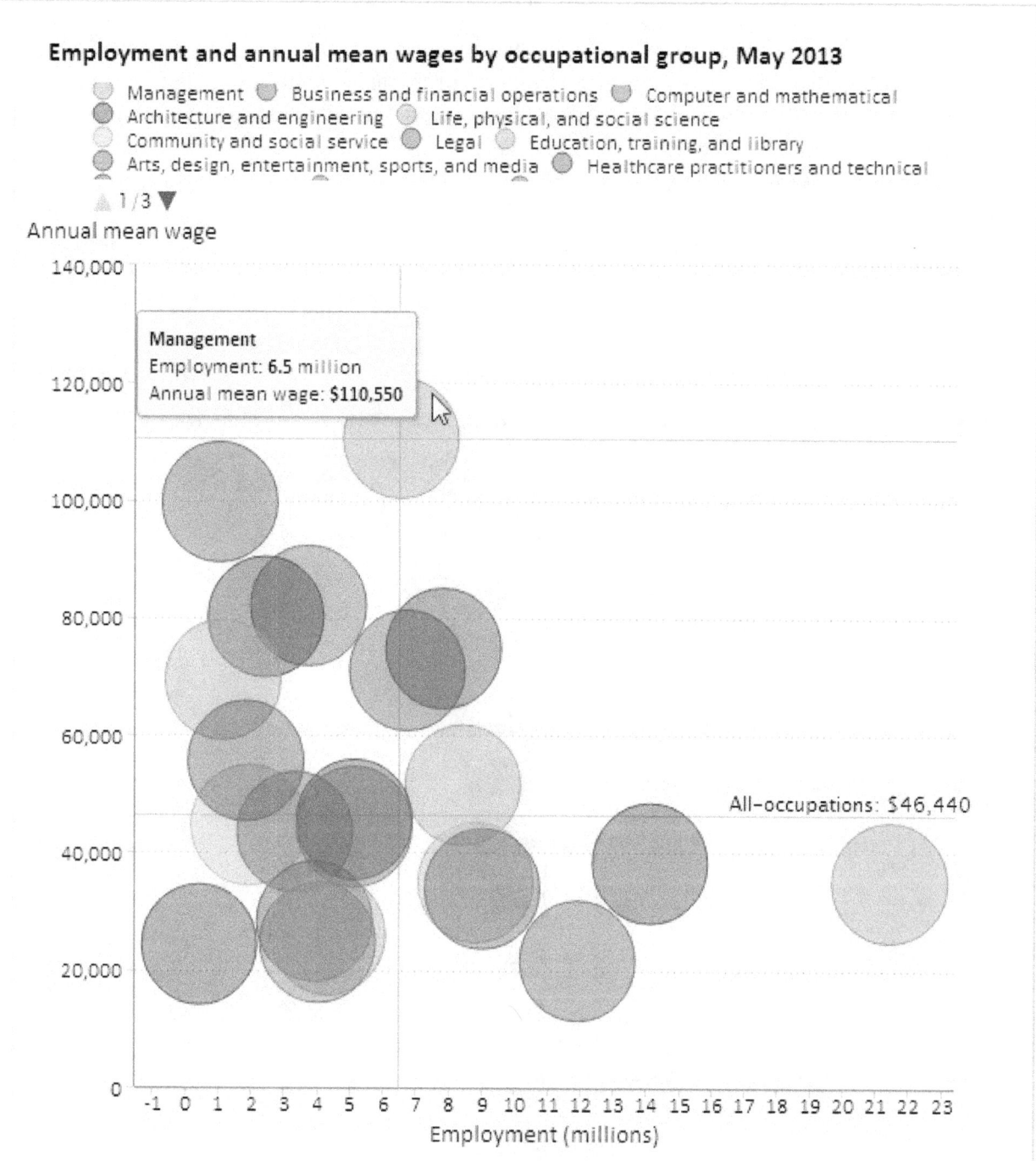

Management Business and financial operations Computer and mathematical
Architecture and engineering Life, physical, and social science
Community and social service Legal Education, training, and library
Arts, design, entertainment, sports, and media Healthcare practitioners and technical

▲ 1/3 ▼

Annual mean wage

Management
Employment: **6.5 million**
Annual mean wage: **$110,550**

All-occupations: $46,440

Employment (millions)

Which occupations had wages near the U.S. average?

Ninety occupations, representing about 10.4 million jobs, had median wages that fell within 5 percent of the all-occupations median of $35,080. Most of these occupations were office and administrative support; construction and extraction; installation, maintenance, and repair; or production occupations. Within these four occupational groups, the largest occupations with median wages near the all-occupations median included bookkeeping, accounting, and auditing clerks; general maintenance and repair workers; and automotive service technicians and mechanics. Dental assistants and self-enrichment education teachers also had wages near the all-occupations median. The median wage represents the wage earned by workers in the middle of the wage distribution, meaning that half of jobs paid less than this amount and the other half paid more.

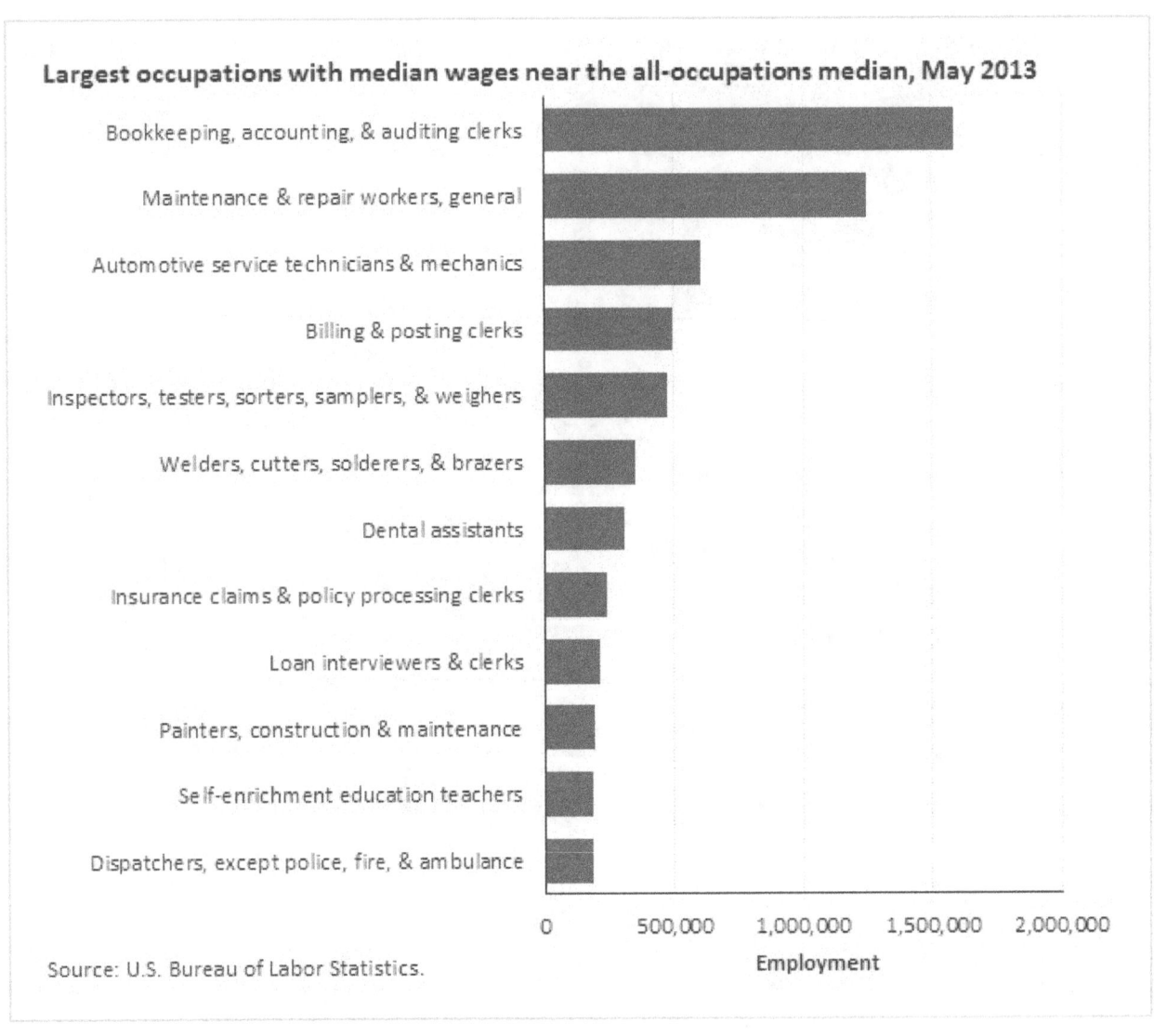

Elementary school teachers was the largest public sector occupation

Local government made up about two-thirds of public sector employment. Five of the 10 occupations with the highest employment in the public sector were teachers or teacher assistants; these occupations were found almost entirely in local government.

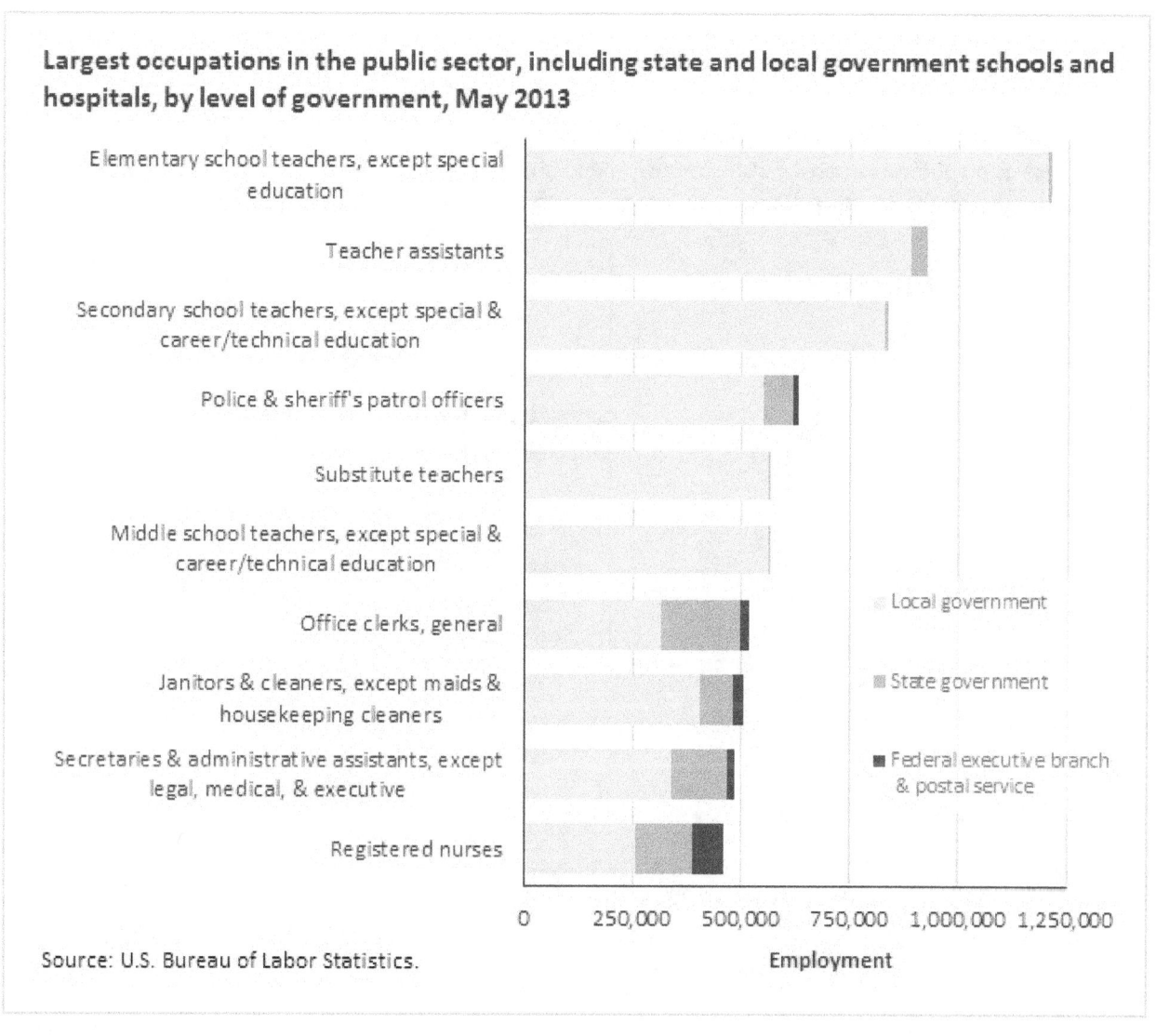

Largest occupations in the public sector, including state and local government schools and hospitals, by level of government, May 2013

Source: U.S. Bureau of Labor Statistics.

Correctional officers was the largest occupation in state government

If state and local government schools and hospitals are excluded, the occupations with the highest public sector employment included police and sheriff's patrol officers, correctional officers and jailers, postal service mail carriers, and firefighters. Of the occupations shown, only postal service mail carriers and all other business operations specialists were found primarily or entirely in federal government. Correctional officers and jailers was the largest occupation in state government, and police and sheriff's patrol officers was the largest occupation in local government.

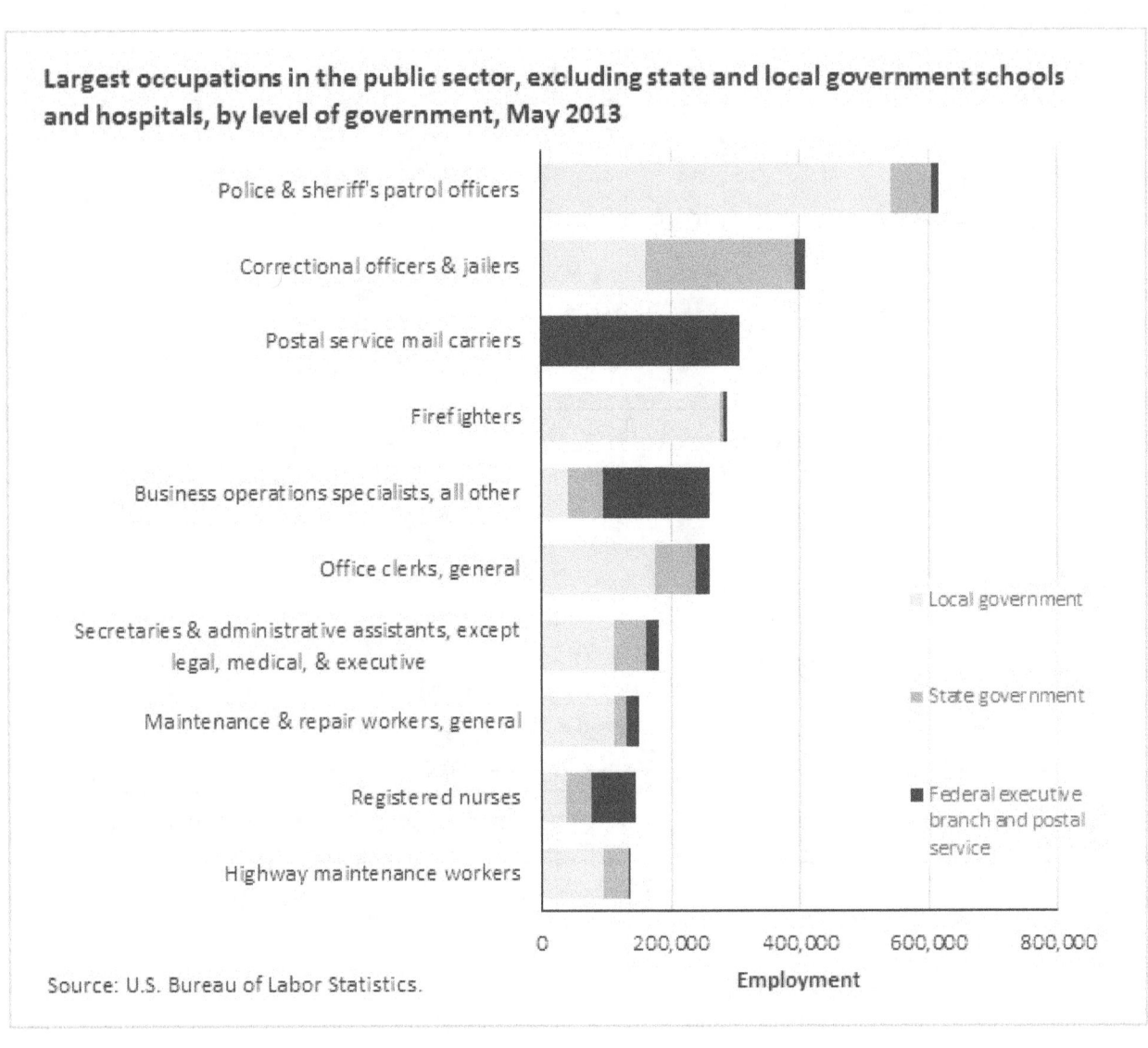

Largest occupations in the public sector, excluding state and local government schools and hospitals, by level of government, May 2013

Source: U.S. Bureau of Labor Statistics.

Nearly two-thirds of employment in occupations typically requiring high school or less for entry

About 39 percent of employment was in occupations that typically required a high school diploma or the equivalent for entry, and another 27 percent of employment was in occupations that typically required less than a high school diploma for entry. Slightly over one-third of employment was in occupations that typically required some type of postsecondary education for entry, with a bachelor's degree the most common type of postsecondary education required.

Typical entry-level educational requirements may differ from the educational attainment of workers currently employed in the occupation because, for example, some workers may have more education than is typically required for entry into their occupations, or the requirements for new entrants may be different from the educational attainment of workers already employed in the occupation.

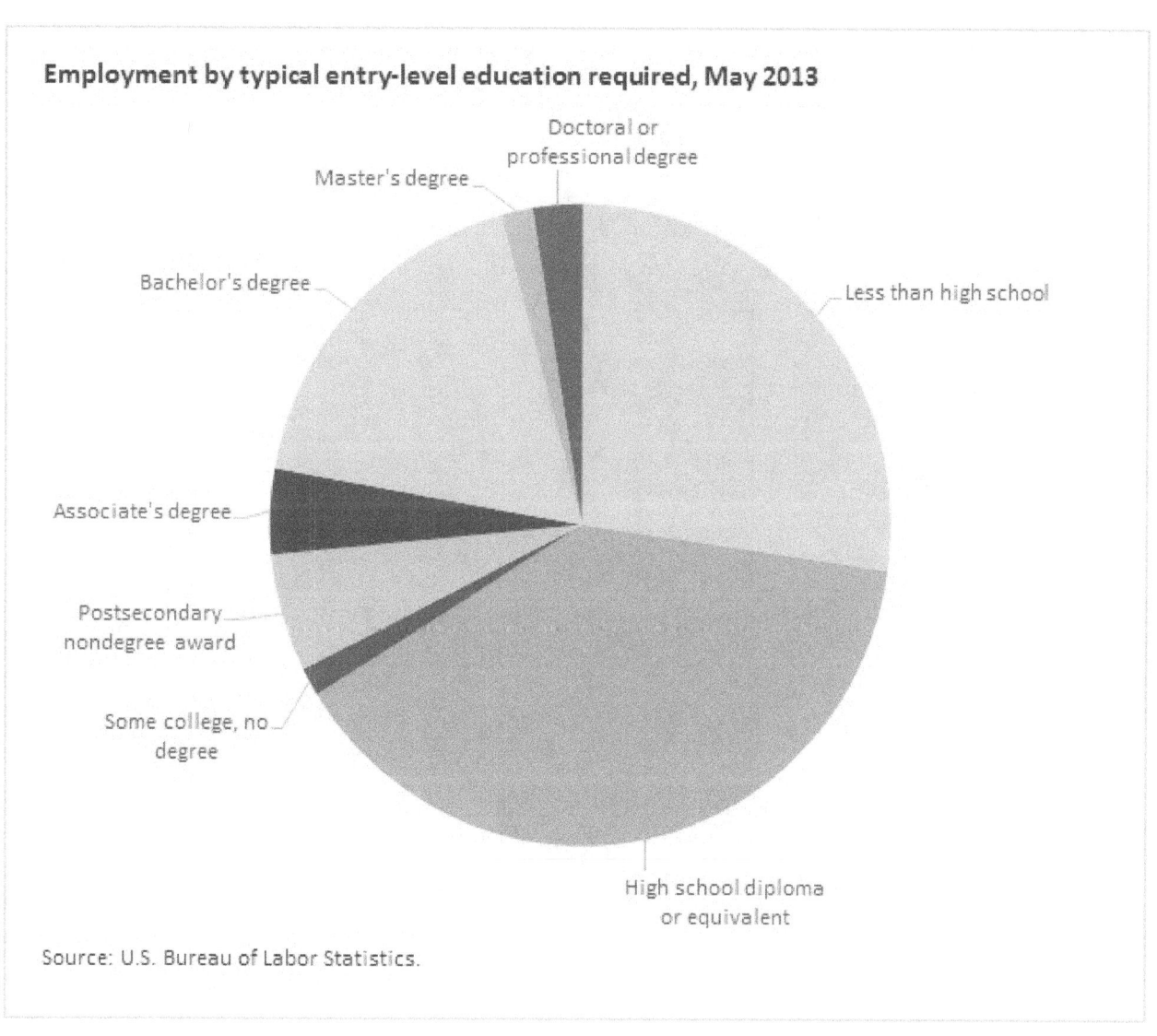

Employment by typical entry-level education required, May 2013

Source: U.S. Bureau of Labor Statistics.

Mean wage of $79,590 for occupations that typically required a bachelor's degree for entry

Average wages were generally higher for occupations that required more education. For example, annual mean wages were $23,840 for occupations typically requiring less than a high school diploma for entry, $41,170 for occupations typically requiring high school or the equivalent, and $60,080 for occupations typically requiring an associate's degree. However, wages did not always rise with higher educational requirements. For example, occupations in the master's degree category paid $9,260 less on average than occupations in the bachelor's degree category. This difference reflects the types of occupations in each educational category. Most of the largest occupations in the master's degree category were associated with education, health care, or community and social service. A number of these occupations had relatively low wages compared with the types of occupations prevalent in the bachelor's degree category.

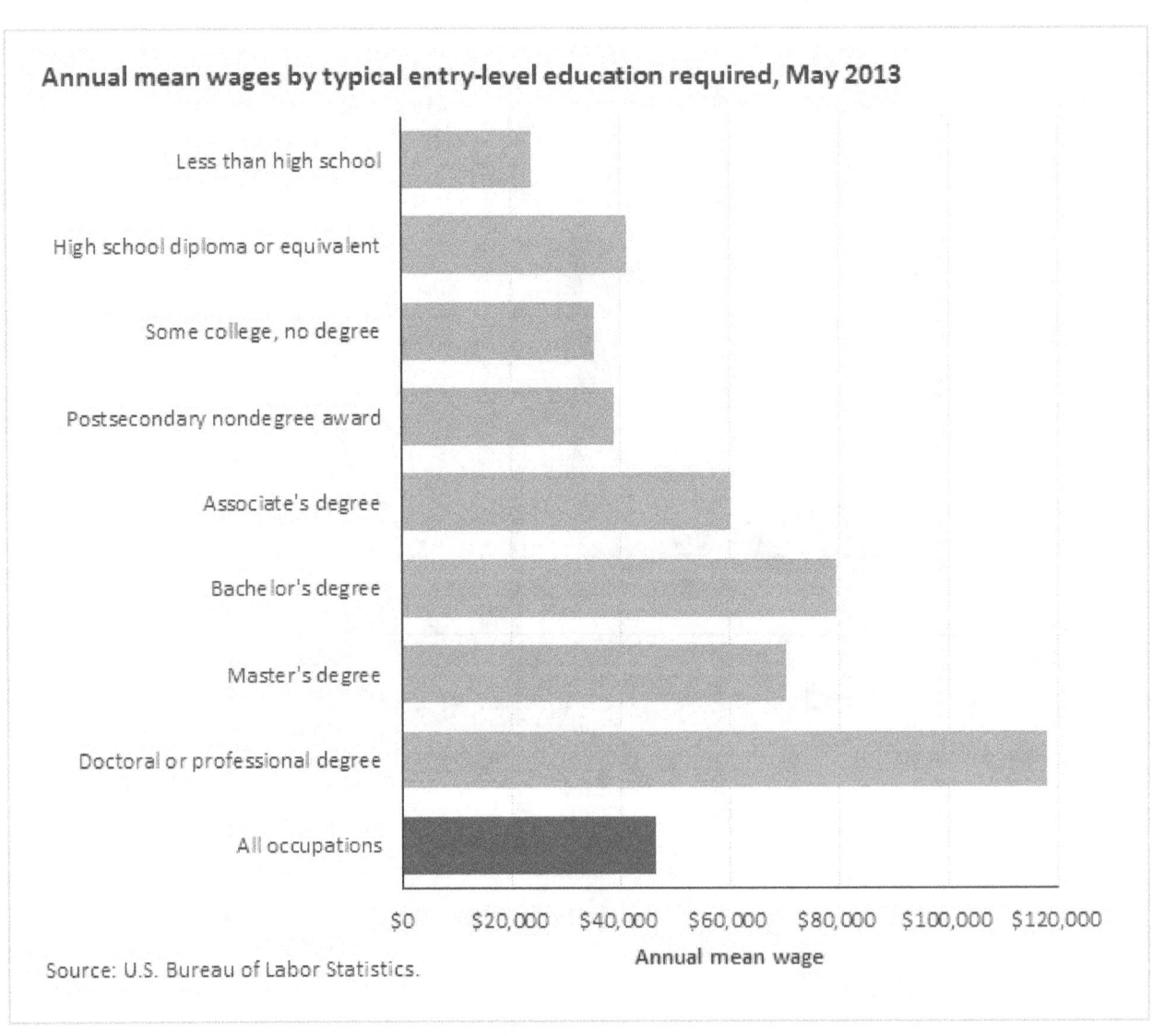

Annual mean wages by typical entry-level education required, May 2013

Source: U.S. Bureau of Labor Statistics.

Highest paying occupations that don't typically require postsecondary education for entry

The annual mean wage was $41,170 for all occupations typically requiring high school or the equivalent for entry, but some individual occupations in this educational category had much higher wages. Several of these were managerial or supervisory occupations. Other high-paying occupations in this educational category were real estate brokers, commercial pilots, and detectives and criminal investigators. Although these occupations did not typically require postsecondary education for entry, most had other requirements to attain competency, such as work experience in a related field, apprenticeship, or moderate- or long-term on-the-job training. In addition, some of these occupations had relatively low employment. For example, gaming managers, nuclear power reactor operators, and power distributors and dispatchers each had fewer than 12,000 jobs nationwide.

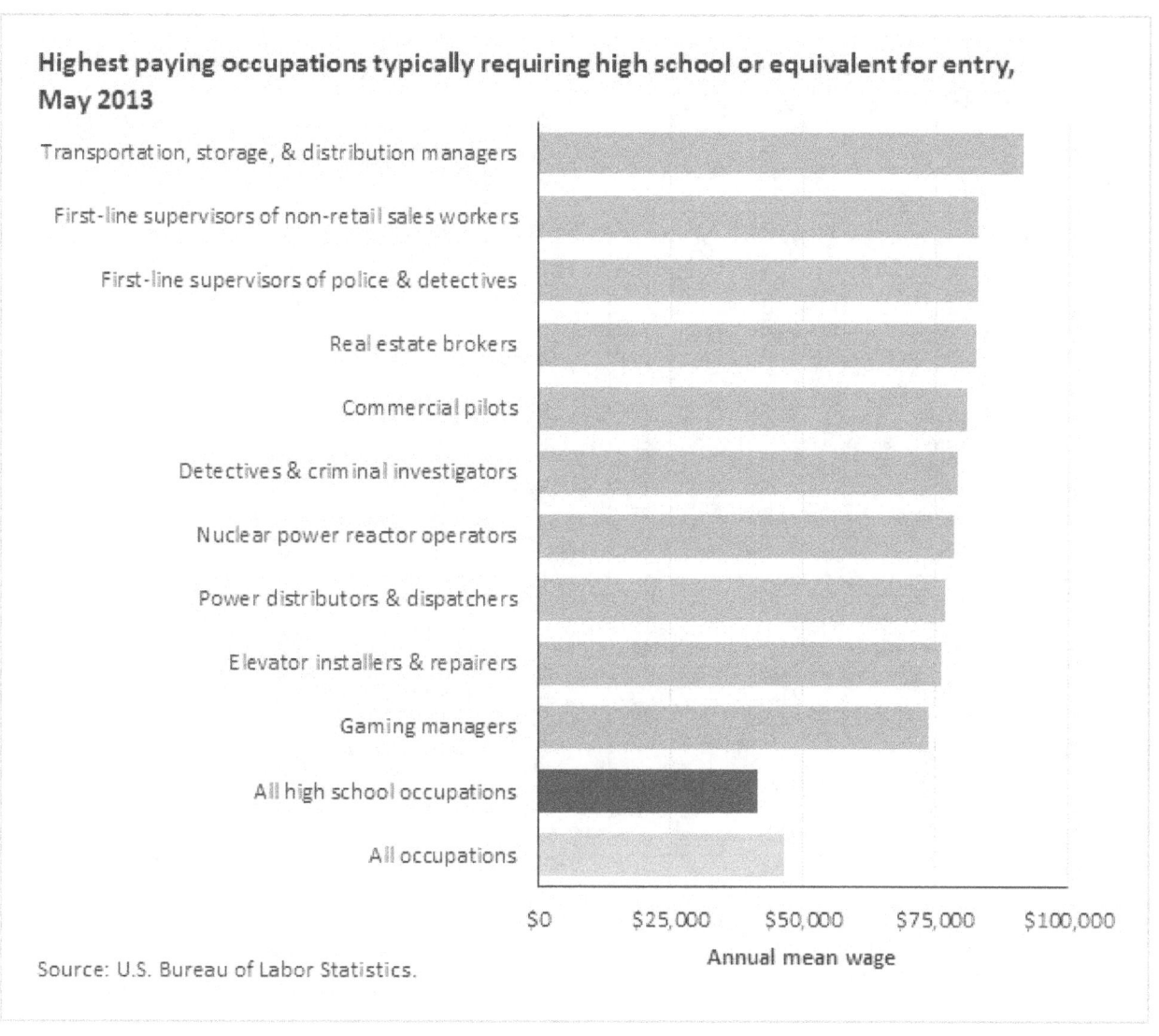

Highest paying occupations typically requiring high school or equivalent for entry, May 2013

Source: U.S. Bureau of Labor Statistics.

Most employment in software publishers was in occupations typically requiring a bachelor's degree

Occupations that typically required a bachelor's degree for entry represented about 18 percent of all employment, but made up the majority of employment in certain industries. These included three industries related to computers and information technology: software publishers, computer systems design and related services, and computer and peripheral equipment manufacturing. Several financial services industries also had high percentages of occupations typically requiring bachelor's degrees for entry. The high educational requirements in these industries were reflected in high wages. Except for elementary and secondary schools, all of the industries shown had mean wages significantly higher than the $46,440 average across all industries, including annual means of over $100,000 in both securities and commodity exchanges and securities and commodity contracts intermediation and brokerage.

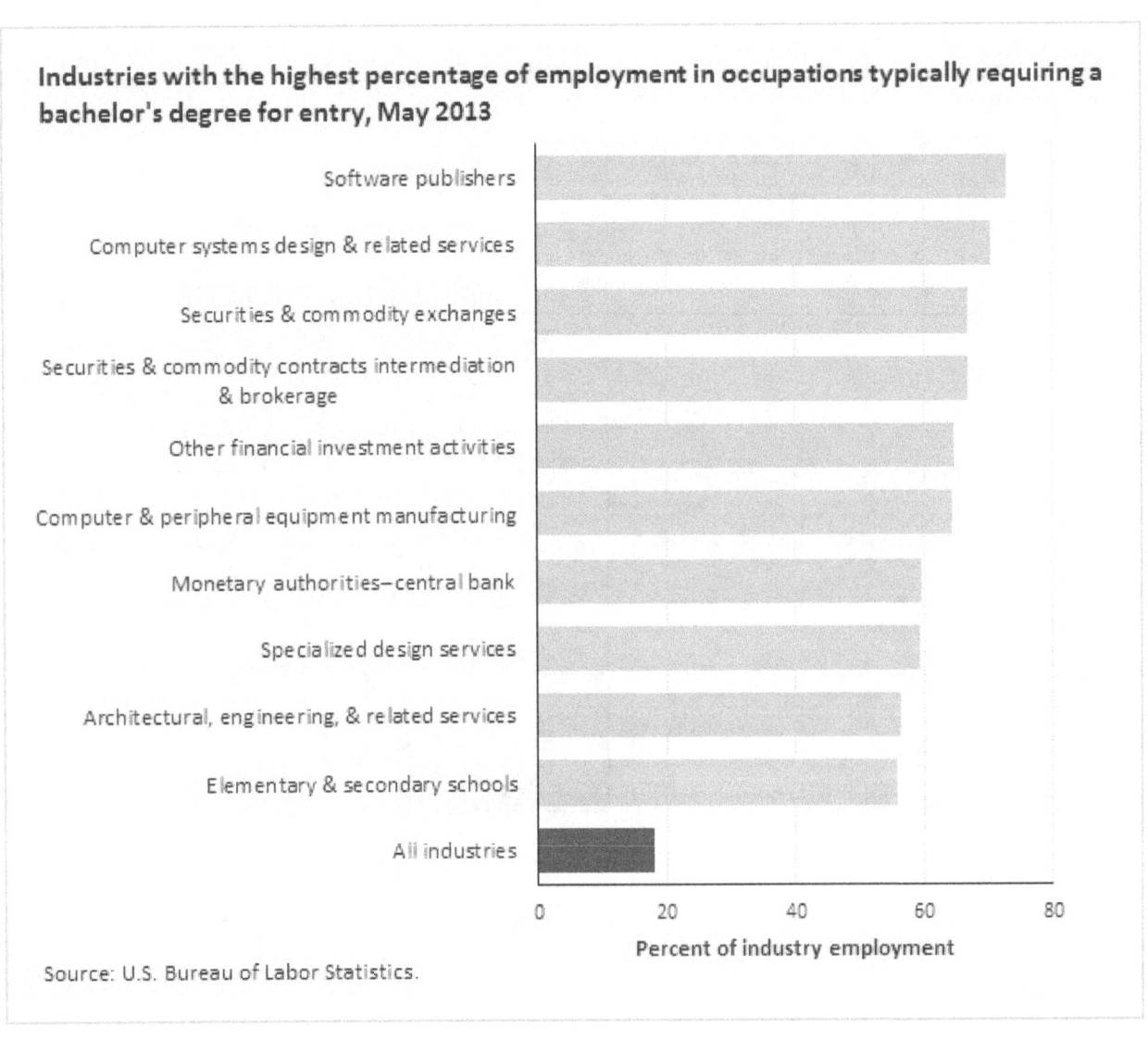

Industries with the highest percentage of employment in occupations typically requiring a bachelor's degree for entry, May 2013

Source: U.S. Bureau of Labor Statistics.

Where were occupations typically requiring a bachelor's degree for entry?

The percentage of jobs in occupations typically requiring a bachelor's degree for entry varied by state, reflecting in part the different mix of industries in each state. Compared with a national average of 18 percent, 32 percent of jobs in the District of Columbia were in occupations that typically required a bachelor's degree for entry. Massachusetts, Virginia, Maryland, and Connecticut each had between 21 and 23 percent of employment in occupations with this educational requirement. At the other end of the spectrum, four states—West Virginia, Louisiana, Mississippi, and Nevada—each had less than 14 percent of employment in occupations that typically required a bachelor's degree for entry.

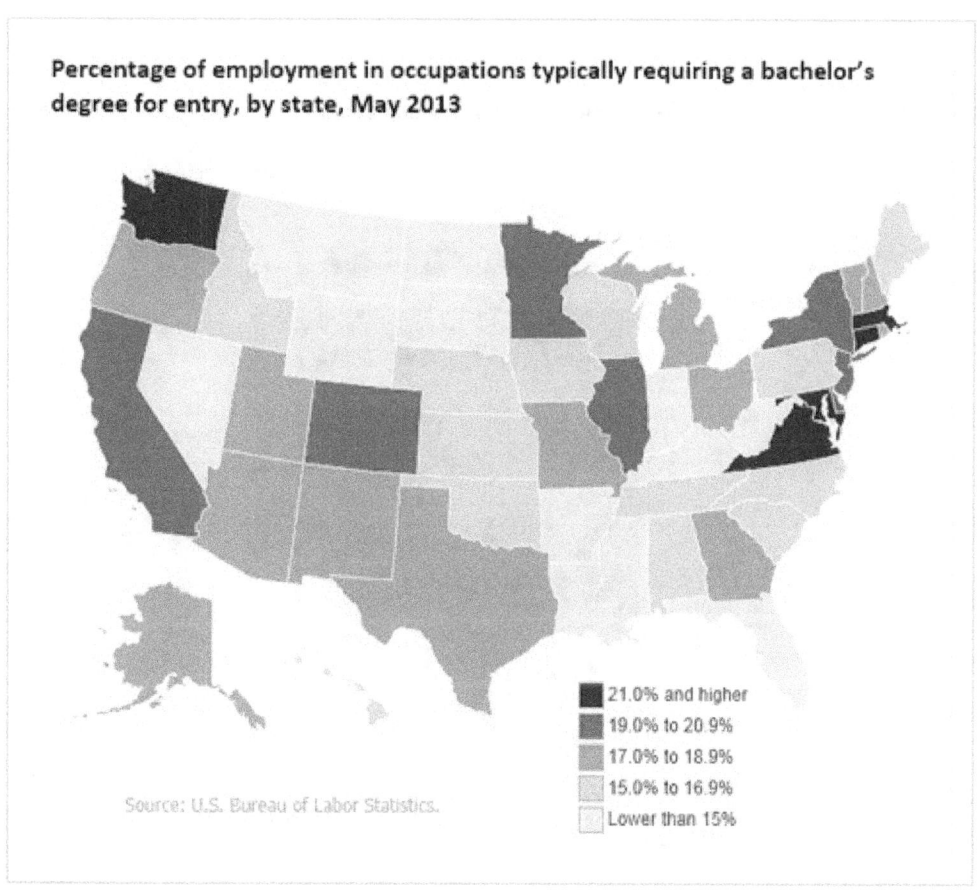

Percentage of employment in occupations typically requiring a bachelor's degree for entry, by state, May 2013

- 21.0% and higher
- 19.0% to 20.9%
- 17.0% to 18.9%
- 15.0% to 16.9%
- Lower than 15%

Source: U.S. Bureau of Labor Statistics.

STEM occupations made up about 6 percent of employment

There were nearly 8.2 million STEM (science, technology, engineering, and mathematics) jobs, making up about 6.2 percent of total U.S. employment. Computer occupations represented the largest subgroup of STEM occupations, making up about 44 percent of total STEM employment. Engineers was the second-largest STEM subgroup. Mathematical science occupations made up less than 2 percent of total STEM employment. Although other definitions of STEM are possible, the STEM occupations group is defined here to consist of 100 different occupations, including computer and mathematical, architecture and engineering, and life and physical science occupations; managerial and postsecondary teaching occupations related to these functional areas; and sales occupations requiring scientific or technical knowledge at the postsecondary level.

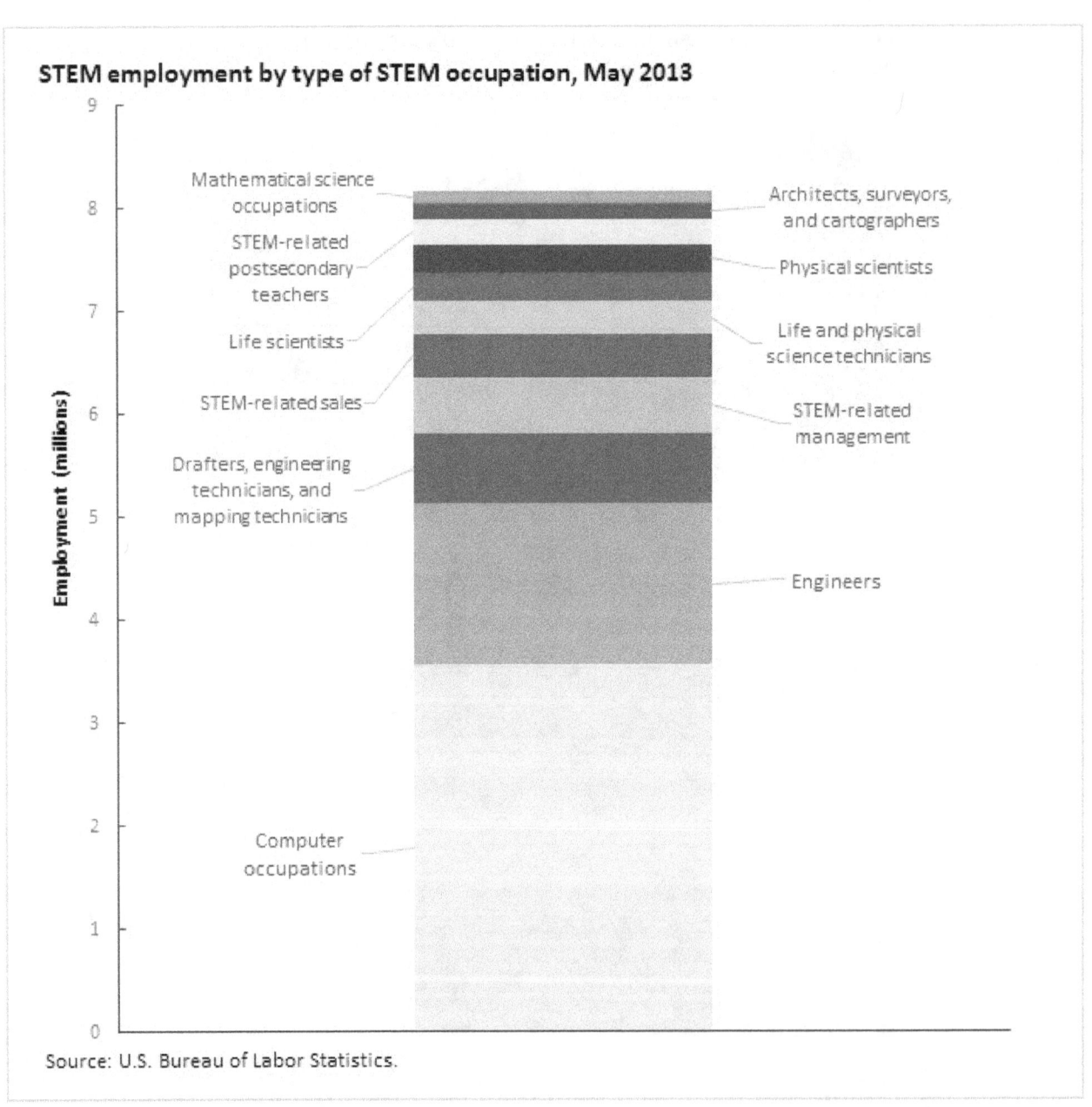

Applications software developers was the largest STEM occupation

Seven of the 10 largest STEM occupations were computer related, including applications software developers, computer user support specialists, and computer systems analysts. Wholesale and manufacturing sales representatives of technical and scientific products was the largest STEM occupation that was not specifically computer related. Civil engineers and mechanical engineers also were among the largest STEM occupations. The smallest STEM occupations (not shown) included mathematical technicians, astronomers, and postsecondary teachers of forest and conservation science, each with employment of less than 2,500.

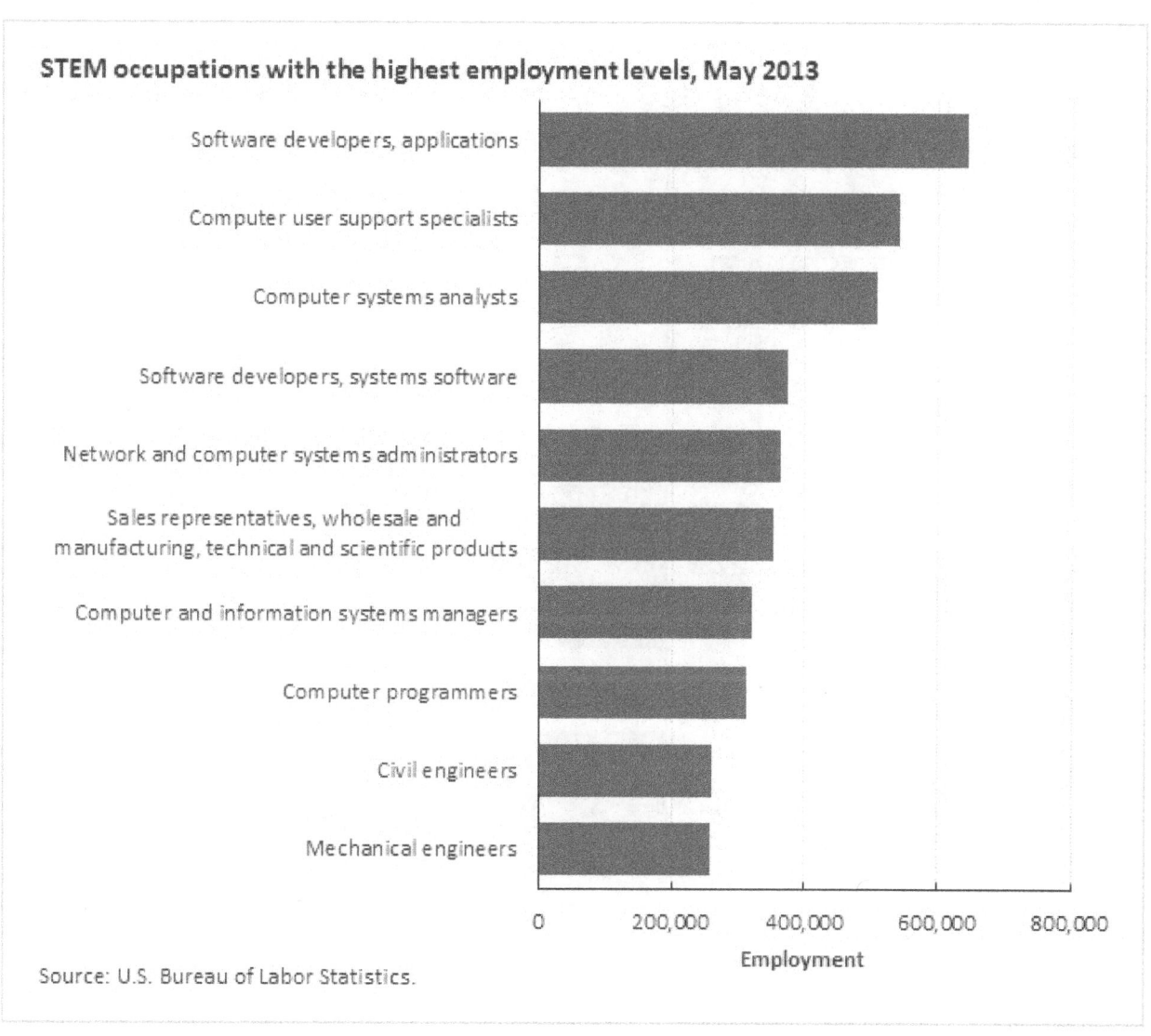

STEM occupations with the highest employment levels, May 2013

Source: U.S. Bureau of Labor Statistics.

STEM occupations had a mean wage of $83,940

Most STEM occupations were high paying: the annual mean wage for STEM occupations was $83,940, compared with $46,440 for all occupations and $43,980 for non-STEM occupations. Only 5 of the 100 STEM occupations had mean wages that were significantly below the all-occupations average; all of these were technician occupations. The highest paying STEM occupations included petroleum engineers, physicists, and the three STEM-related management occupations. High wages for STEM occupations were explained in part by high educational requirements. Nearly all STEM occupations typically required an associate's degree or higher for entry; by comparison, occupations requiring an associate's degree or higher for entry made up only about 27 percent of overall U.S. employment.

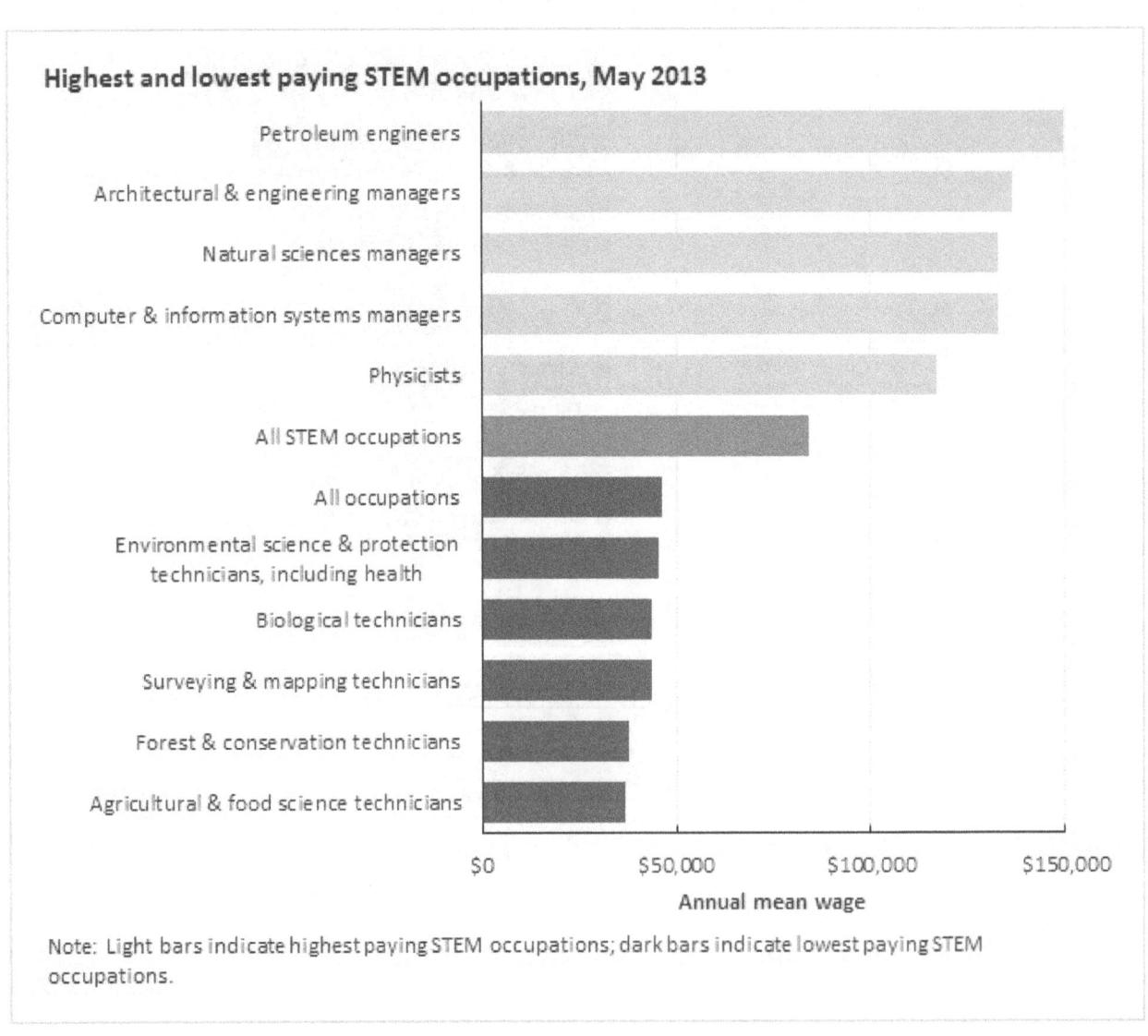

Highest and lowest paying STEM occupations, May 2013

Note: Light bars indicate highest paying STEM occupations; dark bars indicate lowest paying STEM occupations.

STEM occupations made up more than half of employment in some industries

Some industries relied heavily on STEM workers, while other industries had very low concentrations of STEM occupations. Industries with the highest concentrations of STEM employment included computer systems design and related services, with STEM occupations making up about two-thirds of industry employment; architectural, engineering, and related services; software publishers; and several "high-tech" manufacturing industries, such as computer and peripheral equipment manufacturing. Industries with the lowest percentages of STEM employment (not shown) included several retail trade and food service industries, child day care services, and nursing care facilities, each with less than 0.1 percent of industry employment in STEM occupations.

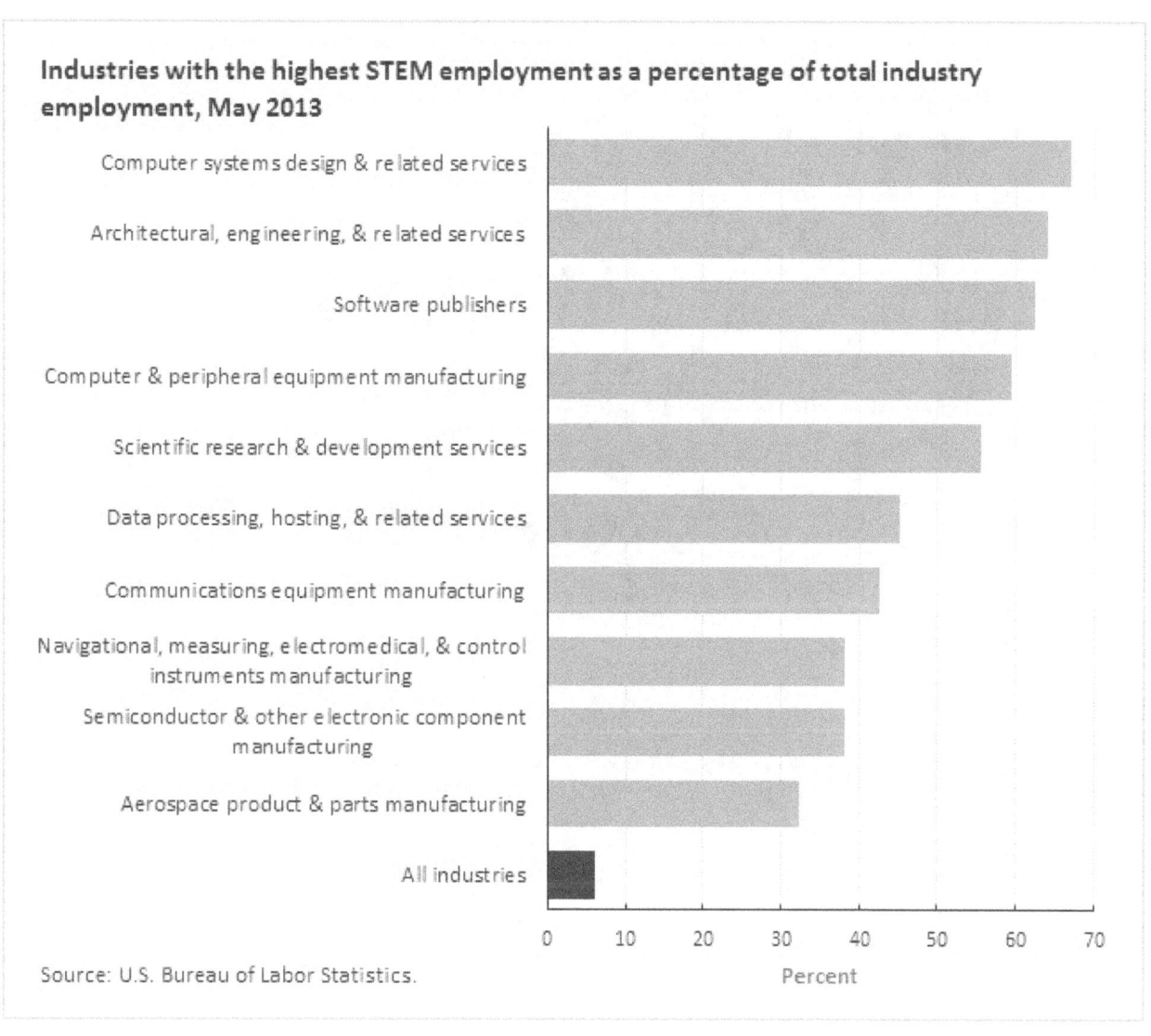

Industries with the highest STEM employment as a percentage of total industry employment, May 2013

Source: U.S. Bureau of Labor Statistics.

Where were STEM occupations most prevalent?

The prevalence of STEM occupations varied geographically. Compared with a national average of 6 percent, over 20 percent of employment in San Jose-Sunnyvale-Santa Clara, California, was in STEM occupations, including high concentrations of computer and information research scientists, electronics engineers, computer hardware engineers, systems software developers, and physicists. Corvallis, Oregon; Boulder, Colorado; and Huntsville, Alabama, each had more than 15 percent of area employment in STEM occupations. STEM jobs made up about 1.5 percent of employment or less in Vineland-Millville-Bridgeton, New Jersey; Brownsville-Harlingen, Texas; Ocean City, New Jersey; and Gadsden, Alabama.

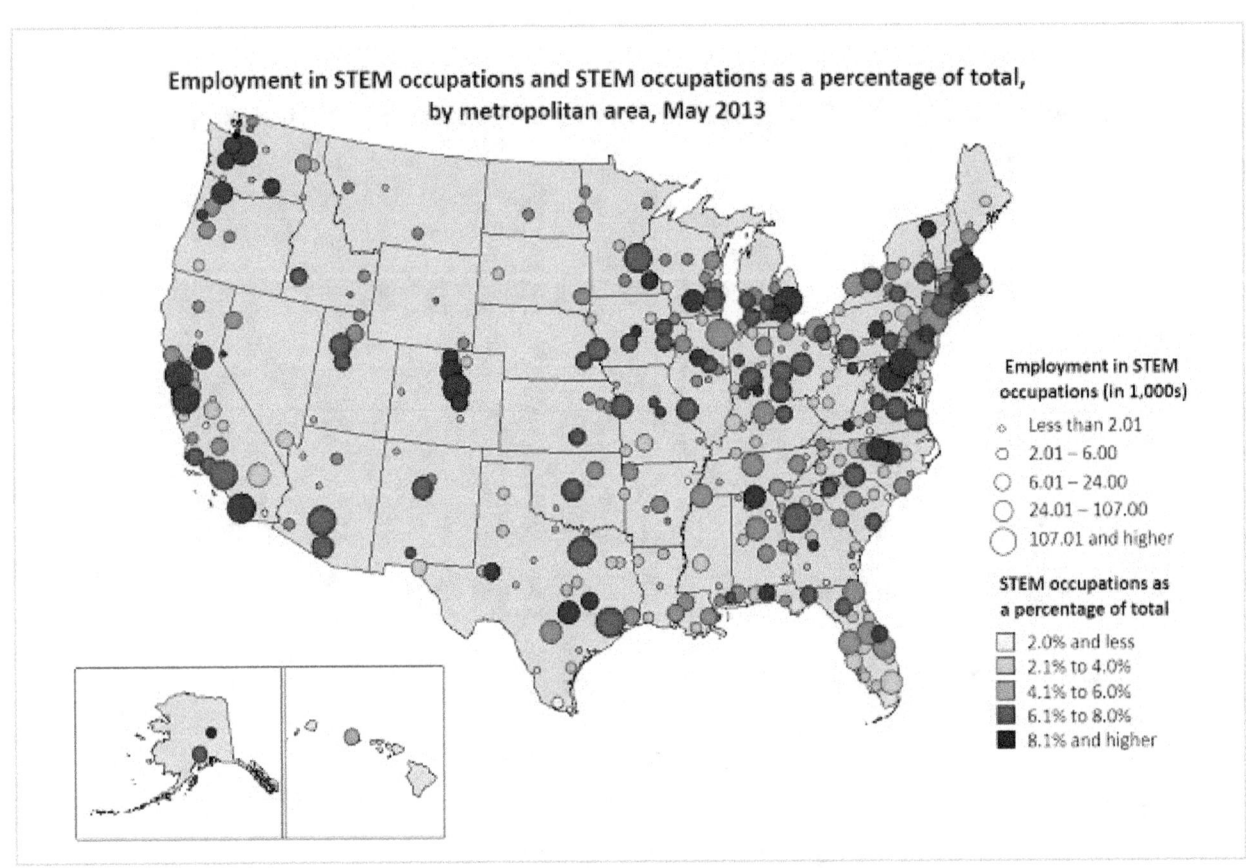

Over 12,000 petroleum engineers were employed in the Houston metropolitan area

Although some STEM occupations, such as computer user support specialists, were spread more evenly across geographic areas, others were highly geographically concentrated. Just over half of all petroleum engineers were found in the 8 metropolitan areas shown in the chart. Petroleum engineers had a location quotient of nearly 56 in Midland, Texas, indicating that petroleum engineers as a percentage of total employment was 56 times as high in Midland as in the U.S. as a whole. Houston-Sugar Land-Baytown, Texas, had one of the highest concentrations of petroleum engineers as well as the highest absolute number of jobs in this occupation (12,520). High employment concentrations didn't always indicate high employment levels, however. Although Casper, Wyoming, had a location quotient of 18.6 for petroleum engineers, this translated into only 210 jobs.

Metropolitan areas with the highest concentrations of petroleum engineers, May 2013

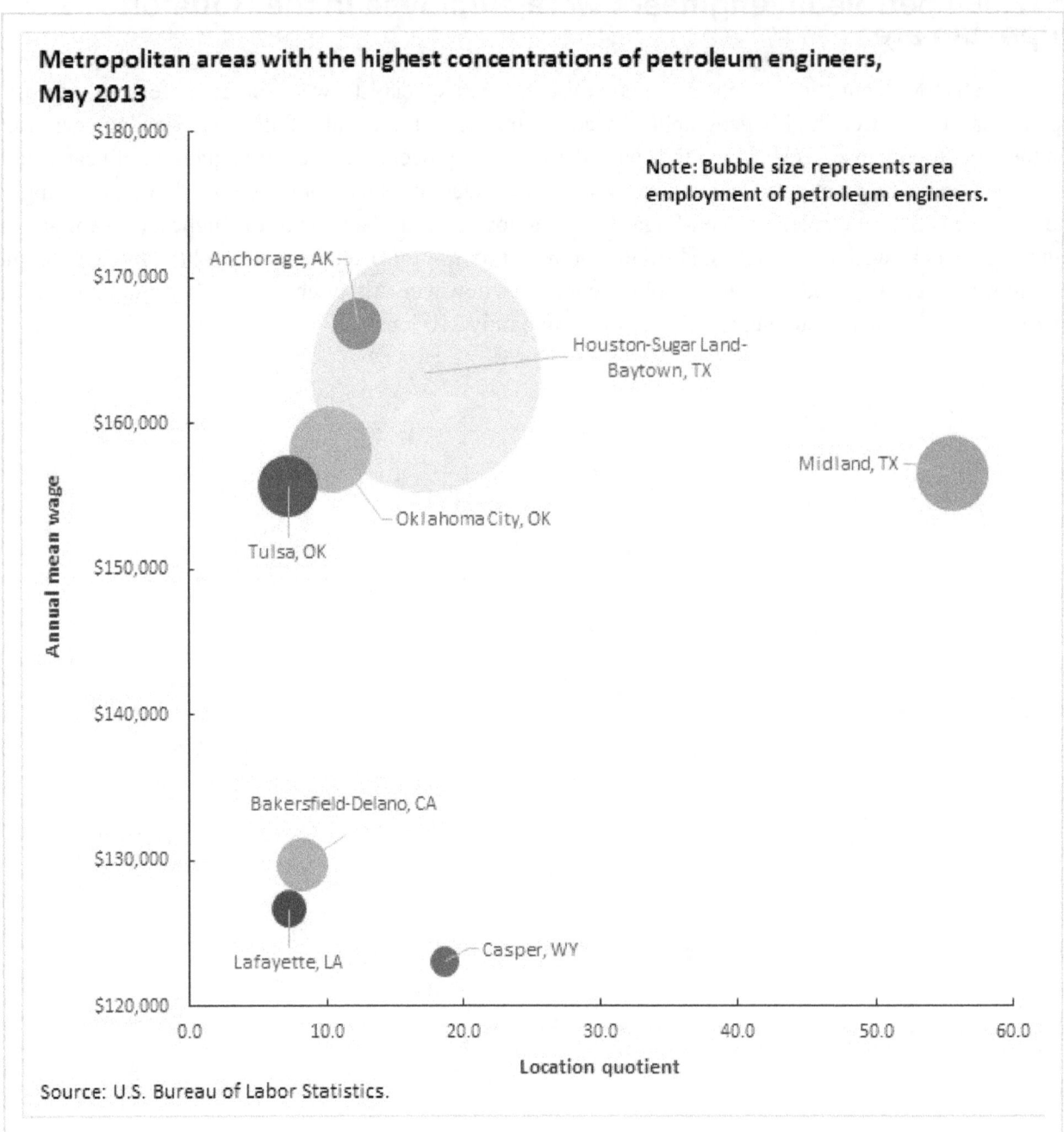

Source: U.S. Bureau of Labor Statistics.

Mining and logging occupations were found primarily in nonmetropolitan areas

About 13 percent of all nonfarm employment was found in nonmetropolitan areas, but nonmetropolitan areas accounted for the majority of employment in certain occupations. Most of the occupations found primarily in nonmetropolitan areas were associated with mining or logging. For example, 74 percent of both mine shuttle car operators and underground mining loading machine operators and 63 percent of mining roof bolters were employed in nonmetropolitan areas. Logging occupations found primarily in nonmetropolitan areas included logging equipment operators, log graders and scalers, and fallers. Outside of mining- and logging-related occupations, the occupations most concentrated in nonmetropolitan areas included slaughterers and meat packers and postmasters and mail superintendents (not shown).

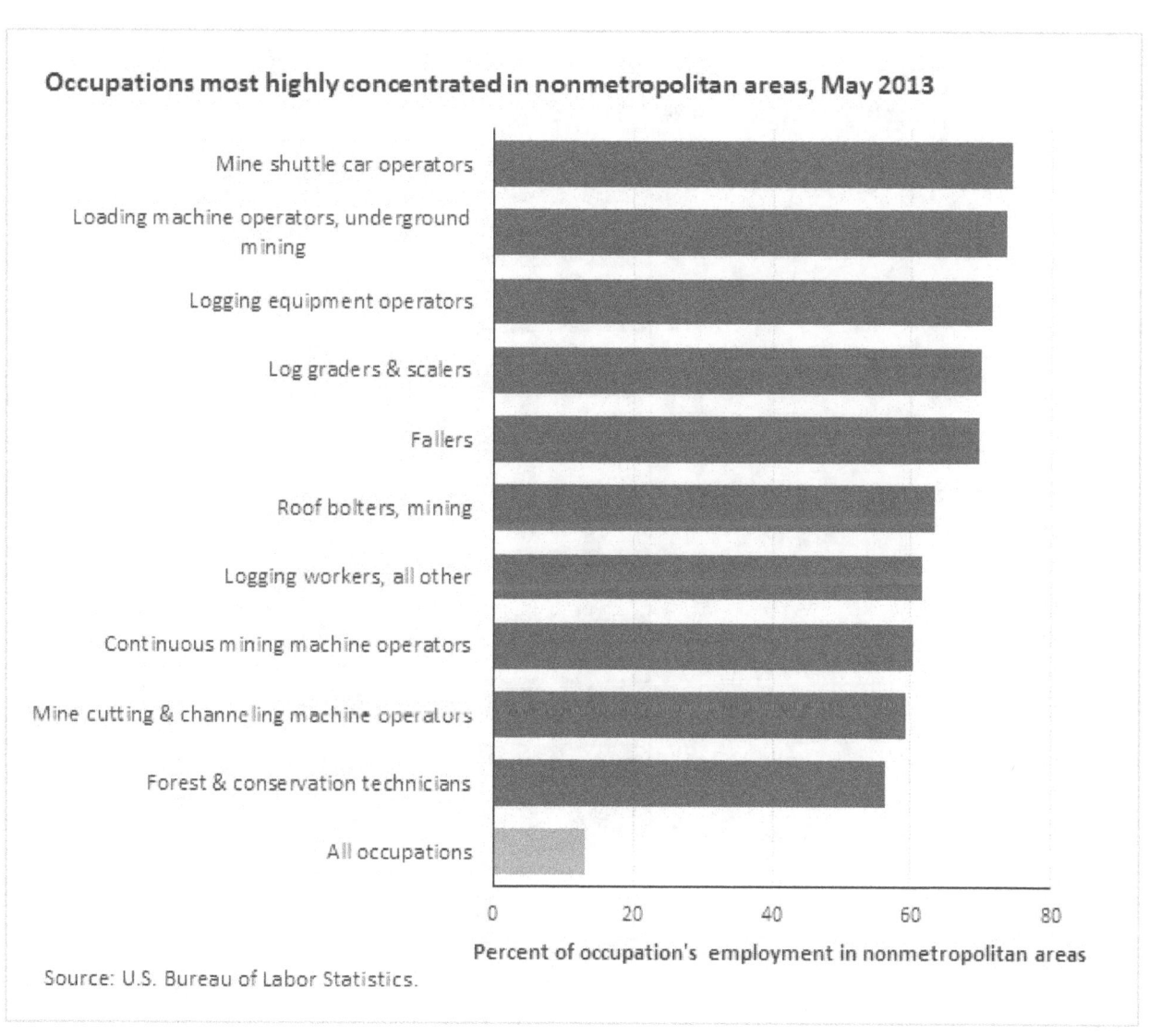

Most political scientists and fashion designers were in large metropolitan areas

Fifteen metropolitan areas had employment of over 1.5 million each in May 2013. These large metropolitan areas made up about 35 percent of total U.S. employment, but an even higher percentage of employment in some occupations. Several of the occupations concentrated in the largest metropolitan areas were related to arts, design, and entertainment, including fashion designers, actors, theatrical and performance makeup artists, and business managers of artists, performers, and athletes. New York-Northern New Jersey-Long Island, New York-New Jersey-Pennsylvania, and Los Angeles-Long Beach-Santa Ana, California, accounted for the majority of employment in these four occupations. Two social science occupations—political scientists and economists—also were concentrated in the largest metropolitan areas, with Washington-Arlington-Alexandria, D.C.-Va.-Md.-W.Va., having the highest employment of both occupations.

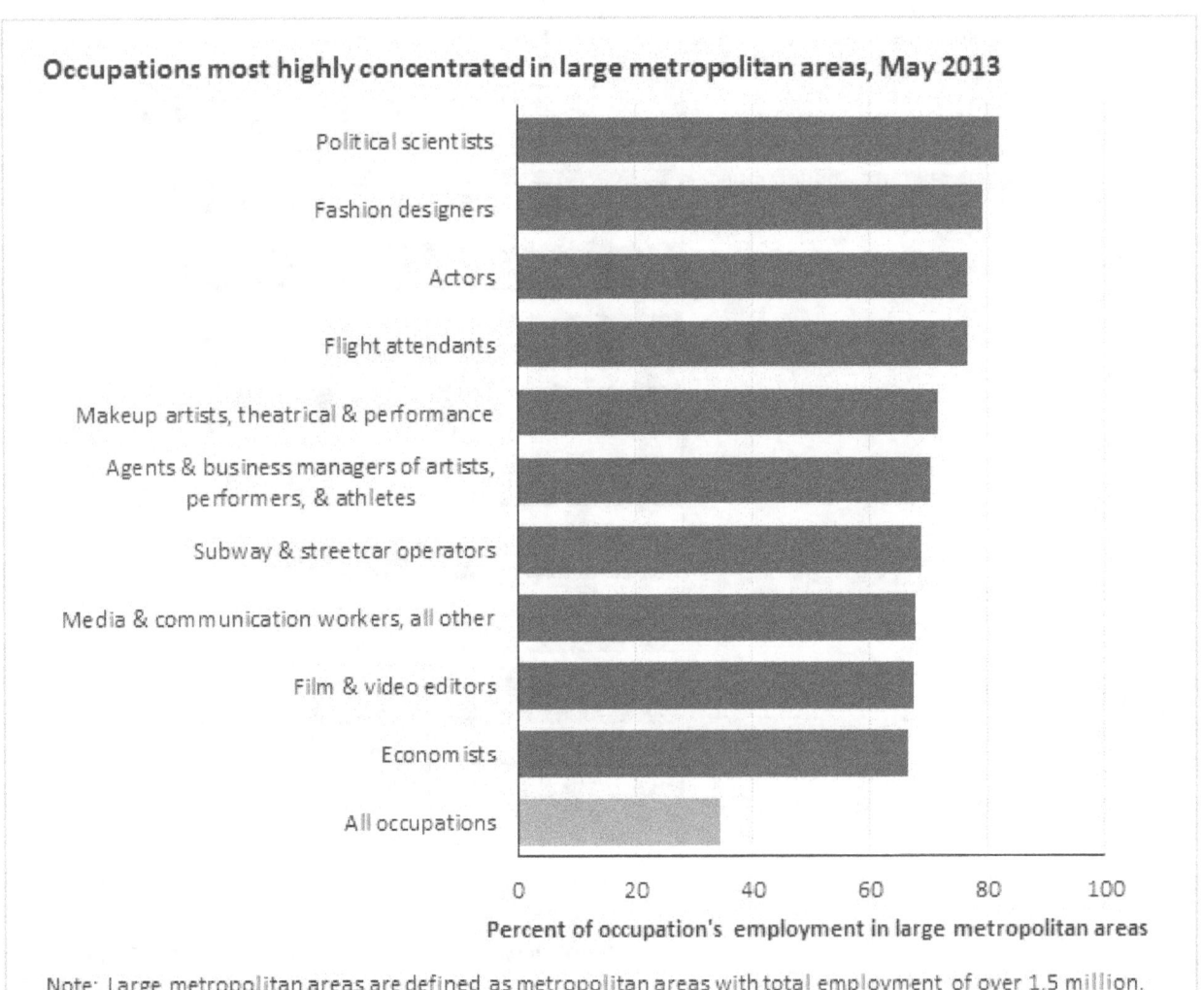

Occupations most highly concentrated in large metropolitan areas, May 2013

Percent of occupation's employment in large metropolitan areas

Note: Large metropolitan areas are defined as metropolitan areas with total employment of over 1.5 million.
Source: U.S. Bureau of Labor Statistics.

More

Audrey Watson is an economist in the Division of Occupational Employment Statistics, U.S. Bureau of Labor Statistics. E-mail: watson.audrey@bls.gov.

The Occupational Employment Statistics (OES) survey is a semiannual mail survey measuring occupational employment and wage rates for wage and salary workers in nonfarm establishments in the United States. OES data available from BLS include cross-industry occupational employment and wage estimates for the nation; over 600 areas, including states and the District of Columbia, metropolitan statistical areas (MSAs), metropolitan divisions, nonmetropolitan areas, and territories; national industry-specific estimates at the NAICS sector, 3-, 4-, and selected 5- and 6-digit industry levels; and national estimates by ownership across all industries and for schools and hospitals. Some of the data used in this Spotlight for employment and wages by typical entry-level education required, STEM occupations, and nonmetropolitan and large metropolitan areas are based on special tabulations of the May 2013 OES data. Publicly available OES data can be found on the OES home page at www.bls.gov/oes/.

Estimates by typical entry-level education required are based on education and training categories assigned by the BLS Employment Projections program. Education and training assignments by detailed occupation are available at www.bls.gov/emp/ep_table_112.htm. Additional charts on the education and training outlook for occupations are available at www.bls.gov/emp/ep_edtrain_outlook.pdf.

This Spotlight uses one of many possible definitions of STEM occupations. Guidance on alternative definitions can be found at www.bls.gov/soc/home.htm#crosswalks.

The STEM data used in this Spotlight are available as a downloadable XLS spreadsheet at www.bls.gov/oes/2013/may/stem.xls.

For more information on STEM occupations, see Science, technology, engineering, and mathematics (STEM) occupations: a visual essay and An overview of employment and wages in science, technology, engineering, and math (STEM) groups.

More information on the geographic distribution of occupations is available in the following articles:

- Occupational employment and wage patterns in nonmetropolitan areas
- Using location quotients to analyze occupational data
- Mapping out a career: an analysis of geographic concentration of occupations